UNCOVERIN
POTENTIALS IN CHILDREN

Alexander Zabadino

Alexander Zabadino

Copyright© 2024 Alexander Zabadino

All rights reserved. No part of this book may be reproduced or transmitted in any form or by any means, electronic or mechanical, including photocopying, recording or by any information storage and retrieval system without prior permission of the author.
This book is a work of non-fiction. The views expressed are solely those of the author, and do not necessarily reflect the views of the publisher and thereby disclaims
any responsibility for them.

Dedicated to God the father, God the Son, and God the Holy Spirit

Contents

INTRODUCTION 8

CHAPTER ONE 14

THE FOUNDATIONS OF ACADEMIC SUCCESS.......14

    What are the foundational needs for unlocking hidden potentials in a child?............................14

CHAPTER 2 22

CHOOSING A SCHOOL FOR YOUR CHILD..............22

    Factors to consider in choosing a good school for your child. 22

CHAPTER 3 32

THE HOME ENVIRONMENT. 32

CHAPTER 4 39

GETTING TO KNOW YOUR CHILD...........................39

    What are the factors to consider in determining the hidden potentials of a child? 42

    Designing an educational program to build interest. 47

    Overcoming weaknesses. 48

    Adapting learning preferences. 49

CHAPTER 5 52

MOTIVATION	52
CHAPTER 6	57
GIFTS AND TALENTS	57
There are things to note about a gift	58
How to discover the gifts and uniqueness in a child.	60
The case study of Albert Einstein.	65
Characteristics of a progressive style of education.	67
CHAPTER 7	71
DISCIPLINE	71
Barriers to effective discipline in children.	73
How to instil discipline in children.	76
CHAPTER 8	81
OVERCOMING CHALLENGES IN CHILDREN	81
Types of educational challenges	81
How to address educational challenges.	88
CHAPTER 9	93
UNRAVELLING THE EXAMINATION PARADOX	93
What are the facts to note about passing an examination?	94

CHAPTER 10 98
WHEN YOU LET GOD TAKE CONTROL. 98
   Revelation of predestination. 100
   The spirit filled parent. 103
   Types of revelation. 108
   The role of prayer in fulfilling the destiny of a child. 113

CHAPTER 11 120
PRAYERS TO DIG OUT HIDDEN POTENTIALS 120
   Prayers for forgiveness and mercy. 120
   Prayers to break evil covenants. 121
   Prayers to break curses. 123
   Prayers to break evil dedication. 125
   Prayers for revelation and guidance. 128
   Prayers for divine favour. 131
   Prayers for wisdom. 133
   Prayers for a retentive memory. 135
   Prayers for good health. 138
   Prayers for regional peace. 141

INTRODUCTION

Academic potential is defined as the inherent virtues for manifestation, or the capabilities that a child has, that is locked up inside them. However, a child may be loaded with potentials, but the parents may be unable to unlock the potentials in order that that it would manifest, and the child would not be able to succeed in life. A child may be living with the parents and enrolled in school, but may not perform well academically or otherwise. However, if that child is taken to another school or area, where the environment or curriculum shift, then the potentials are unlocked, and success begins in bounds.

To consider nurturing a child for academic success, there is a foundation to be laid, and a preparation to be made, as these factors enhance the learning experience. The family that the child comes from has to be a peaceful and supportive one, and the environment where the child intends to study must be a peaceful one as well. The parents must be prepared to finance the education of the child. Many parents enrol their ward in expensive schools which are at the end of the day, they cannot afford, and may not deliver quality education. The provision of a good education for a child is a collective responsibility of both parents and teachers.

The truth is that it is impossible to unlock virtues or potentials that is inside a child, if the parent does not know if the child has a virtue, or the nature of such. The parents of the child have a great role to play in observing a child, knowing clearly, this is what my son likes, and this is what he is capable of doing, or would be able to do. Many children grow up in life dilly-dallying, not knowing exactly what they are cut out to do. It is needful for a parent to be aware of the unique abilities of a child.

The choice of school that a child is enrolled also affects the attainment of the academic potentials of the child. Contrary to what many people think, the most expensive schools might not be able to bring out the best in a pupil! The alignment to the perceived educational and developmental needs of the child, schedule of the school, adherence to schedule, discipline in the school, and results of the pupils in external examinations, are some of the factors to consider.

The home environment also has some impact in unlocking the academic potentials of a child. An unstable, unsettled and chaotic home environment, where parents are always at war against one another wouldn't support study at home. Misunderstandings between both parents, and insecurities in the home front, would a have negative impact in the unlocking of a child's academic potentials, in a physical or emotional sense.

It must be put into consideration that spiritual factors too, need to be addressed. The spirit realm rules the physical, and spiritual things affect the physical performance of a child, and the ability to be able to unlock academic potentials. The relationship between the mind and the body is not only applicable to health, but also learning. If the mind is troubled, it would be difficult to achieve great things academically.

It is therefore pertinent to take spiritual steps in unlocking the potentials of a child. Curses, evil covenants, evil dedication, demonic influence and the problem of repeated sickness, strange behaviour and poor mental health, are just but a few. A child who is always under attack in the night, seeing and hearing what others can't, would get to class the next day and sleep. Due to a negative aura, learning is affected. Whichever way you view it, such a child needs urgent spiritual attention under these circumstances.

Reduced motivation is one of those factors that prevents a child from becoming the best that they could possibly be. This could be due to different factors in the life of the child, socially, in the family or even in the school. This goes a long way to reduce focus, attention and concentration to studies in the child, which eventually affects how you can bring out the best in a child. There should be a rapport between the parents and teachers at a closer level, to discuss the problems of the child, tackle challenges, and make learning easier.

When it comes to electronic learning and engagement, there is a lot to benefit from. There are apps, to learn languages, solve mathematical problems, and others. ChatGPT offers answers to any questions the student or parents may have.

Platforms like Moodle, Canvas, Google classroom, eBooks, educational YouTube channels and robots are just to mention a few of the options that are available.

Academic tests and measurements could be controversial sometimes when it comes to measuring academic capabilities and achievements. Sometimes, exams may not ensure the academic ability of a child accurately. The way a measuring instrument (examination questions) is presented can bring a twist. It is very important for a child to be groomed on how to respond to questions of a particular external exam. The marking g scheme should be thoroughly discussed with the child. If you are normally required to write an answer with the units, then you should know this before the exams.

This book discusses the various associated problems, pertinent to unlocking academic potentials in children. The chapters following discuss all the problems mentioned, and how to solve them. This book is a valuable asset to parents and teachers, as well as teenagers who can read and understand the contents and apply them to solving individual or collective problems. Every child is loaded with potentials, but it requires a good parent, time and painstaking hard work, to recognise and unlock the potentials towards the success and fulfilment of the child. The book no doubt, prepares the child for a powerful future.

CHAPTER ONE

THE FOUNDATIONS OF ACADEMIC SUCCESS

There is always a beginning, and a foundation on which every good thing is built upon, and achieving a high academic potential requires a foundation as well. By this we mean preparations and things necessary in order to have a seamless learning experience and maximum potentials and success. It does not really matter the quality of education, if these factors are not present and planned into the life of the child, maximal academic potentials may not be achieved. The following considerations come before any others.

What are the foundational needs for unlocking hidden potentials in a child?

Establish a supportive environment.

A good environment offers support in every way, and ensures serenity and calmness, and promotes a desire to learn. The result is there is a limit to distractions, and the child is able to concentrate better. In the classroom or be it at home, the study space should be well arranged with the necessary things like pens, chalk, dusters and others well arranged. The furniture should not be too high or too low, and ergonomic considerations should be employed. The environment does not probably mean the physical environment, but also psychological and emotional factors should be taken into consideration in supporting a child. The student should be free from all distractions and should not be overburdened by disagreements between the parents at home, or even disputes in the school environment between teachers, or other categories of staff.

Develop study habits.

In order to develop a study habit, a timetable is necessary at home or in school for the student to work with. On arrival from school, students should be taught to study, and possibly a private teacher could be engaged for about two hours, say between 4pm - 6pm. Further studies could be done for another one hour before or after dinner.

This should be a consistent practice, irrespective of what happens, it should be followed religiously as much as possible. The schedules could also be reviewed.

Setting of goals.

Goals should be set and time frames should attach to tasks. There also should be a quantum of work that should be done within a period of time. This discourages indolence and stimulates the child to work continuously, thereby bringing the best out of the child. The goals should be achievable for age and experience. Goals should be broken down to smaller bits to make them more achievable. If you had planned that a child should read a full book for a year. However, you feel he or she may not be able to read and understand effectively, you could do a chapter per month, instead of setting the child's mind on the goal of studying 12 chapters for the year.

Learn to stimulate the intellect and curiosity.

It is not just sufficient for a child to study and learn by going through the pages of the book. An attempt should be made to stimulate the intellect of the child by asking questions in various twists about what he or she has read. For example, if a particular topic that the child is currently studying is repeated in a higher class, you may give just one question or two from that of the higher class. This promotes curiosity and critical thinking. Practical projects should be introduced to stimulate curiosity which may also be a bit complex occasionally.

Always be sensitive to emotions.

One of the foundations that must be laid is that of sensitivity to emotions, in order to bring out the best in a child. Children are reserved and may be shy, especially if they are studying in an unfamiliar environment. Then there should be sensitivity to their mood, and the teacher or patent should learn to interpret their moods, or emotions, and act appropriately. The child may be sad, or hungry and uncooperative, and when you notice this, you could tell him or her to go eat something, or give a break. The child is then refreshed and is better on resumption of the break.

Play.

Children love to play, but yet when they play, you could design it as a form of extracurricular activity, so that the experience they have could be useful on the overall analysis. A game of "snakes and ladders" could be categorised as play, as well as an extracurricular activity. It is also a way of encouraging team work and creativity. Extracurricular activities also include sports, baking, carpentry. Welding and many others. Extracurricular activities promote physical and emotional health.

Good health.

Good health is a condition for full concentration of a child, during studies. A child that that for example has tommy ache, headache, or has a cough won't be able concentrate and learn. This is why it is good to think about disease prevention at all times in children, as well as immediate attention and care, whenever a child falls sick. A healthy and balanced diet, with exercises are further good ways of enhancing the health of a child.

Sleep.

A good night sleep rests the brain of a child and enhances concentration and learning. It is also helpful during the day for a child to be given the opportunity to sleep, when they are tired. Sleep helps to repair worn out tissues and enhances good health. Sleep strengthens the immune system, brain development, problem solving, attention and focus, emotional and social health, and generally the health of the child.

Liaison with teachers.

Parents should try to meet with the teachers, personally to discuss the progress of the child. Teachers too should be eager to discuss the progress of the child. They should also be willing to know the problems of the child, and how they could solve these problems in school or at home. The progress made should be discussed on regular basis between the parents and teachers.

A mind-set that enhances growth.

As a result of this they should not only be willing to celebrate effort put in by the student, but should be willing to celebrate progress, and subsequently the overall progress. On a general view, there are parents/teachers association meetings. All parents should endeavour to attend and be active in these meetings asking questions where necessary. Little successes should be celebrated, as a motivational measure.

Consistency.

No matter the amount of resources that are available, and the quality of school the child attends, still, every effort that is being made need to be consistent, otherwise, there will be no tangible results. However, if the child is consistent in studying and using a special strategy every time without overlooking any subject, then the results will be excellent. During the holidays, the children should continue studying consistently. A lot of students relax during the holidays and drop in performance.

CHAPTER 2

CHOOSING A SCHOOL FOR YOUR CHILD

Choosing a school for a child might look simple, but it's an area, where most parents are vulnerable to mistakes, only to discover much later in the educational journey of a child that they have made a wrong decision which does not agree with the needs and development of the child. The right school for your child should align with academic, social, and emotional needs and development of a child, before the academic potentials can be fully unlocked. Sub-qualified and inexperienced teachers, the wrong educational environment, or lack of appropriate facilities wouldn't fully unlock the academic potentials of your child. Let us now look at the factors to consider in choosing a good school for your child.

Factors to consider in choosing a good school for your child.

Distance from home.

One of those things that would ensure that a child gets the best from a school, that many parents would fail to realise, is the distance from the house, where student lives. A student who travels daily to school, and travels back, spending a couple of hours on the way, would likely be stressed, exhausted, on getting to school, affecting attention and focus in class. It takes time to fully settle in class, and to concentrate. At the end of the term, quite a lot of time intended for classroom activities would have been lost. There's also very little time to spend upon closing from school in the afternoon, because a lot of time would have been spent travelling back home, and the child would be very tired. When the school is near, it is also easy to monitor the progress of a child, as a parent and be aware of what is happening in the school.

Curriculum.

The Curriculum is the subjects or disciplines that are being taught per class, and the period used to teach the subjects. Most schools have open days that prospective parents could walk in to know more about the subjects and the rationale behind the teaching of those subjects. Parents who have wards in the school already could also walk in to check the performance of their children. In some schools you could book an appointment and walk in to assess the Curriculum. This should entail core academic subjects, and also extracurricular concerns, based on the interests and needs of the child.

Teaching approach.

There are different teaching approaches, and learning must be flexible in order to maximally unlock the academic potentials in a child. In much younger children, the best approach is to use an interactive approach, which engages their minds, often incorporating questions and answers, to stimulate curiosity and creativity. The children should also be allowed to embrace some elements of play, along the line. In older students, in the secondary schools, it should be more structured and depend on the specific subject requirements.

When enrolling a child of between two to ten years, then we should be looking at a creative approach. However, for a child who is eleven and above, we should look at a more independent and structured approach. A good school must be able to utilise these approaches depending on the age of the child.

Teacher to student ratio.

The fewer the number of students in a class, the better the teacher student ratio, and the better the individual attention given to a student. This means that it is easier to deal with a student individually with a more focused approach, making it easier to engage, impact knowledge, and unlock academic potentials. Over time, this is a very good facility. There are schools that only take a maximum of twenty students per class. They might end up employing more teachers, paying more in terms of salary, and charging a higher school fee. It is however worth it.

School culture.

A very important consideration in choosing a school is the school culture. This refers to other strong points that characterise the school, that they are known for. This starts from the religious inclinations of the school. Does it agree with your religious inclinations? In spite of all these, is there discipline in the school. Discipline is one of the factors that bring the best out of a child, and it must be enforced. An undisciplined child will never be motivated to study, and wouldn't be consistent in the pursuit of academic excellence. It is also important for the school to Foster a sense of community, by having groups, and by celebrating diversity, making students to accept and respect the views of other students.

Academic results in external exams.

One major factor that sets a school apart amongst others, is not the individual student's performance in their school, but the results of the school in external exams, when compared to other schools, especially a number of years. If they consistently rank high in performance, then it means the school is a good school. It is possible for a school to award marks liberally, and that seemingly makes it look as if the students are good. Performance in external exams often show the quality of the curriculum and teaching approach.

Tuition and overall costs.

The cost of education per year is something to seriously consider. The right type of education must be affordable, not just in one instance, but over a number of years. Inability to settle your bills consistently might result into kicking your child out of school. Even when the tuition is free, inability to meet up with other petty needs might have devastating emotional consequences on your child. There may be some schools that offer scholarships, which may be an option for families in need. There is however a mystery. It is that good quality education for your child might not cost a fortune! My children attended schools that didn't cost a fortune, but performed excellently well.

Prayer.

The place of prayer cannot be underestimated when it comes to choosing a school for a child. It is important to pray continuously until you receive a reply. The reply will usually come in form of a dream, as we have in Job 33:15-16. It states that "in a dream, in a vision of the night, when deep sleep falleth upon men, in slumberings upon the bed, then he openeth their ears, and sealeth their instruction. At other times, it will be through an inner knowing, and agreement with your spirit. Also, it may be through a happenstance leading to a knowledge of the truth. Furthermore, you may hear an audible voice. When you pray and God reveals to you, it is certain that the school will meet the needs of your child, and satisfy most of the things stated above.

Special needs.

Students may have learning disabilities that may impact learning negatively. The availability of support services for special needs is desirable. These include special educational programs, specialist teachers, assisting technology like text-to-speech, speech therapy, occupational therapy, behaviour therapy and mental health support should be available.

School facilities and resources.

There are some standard facilities that a school should have. These include a sports arena, for games like football, basketball, volleyball, or others. A school should have a library, as well as laboratories. Science students need laboratories. There should also be a language laboratory, a school clinic, and other little things like a first aid box, and fire extinguishers. The classrooms also should be large, adequately furnished, and well ventilated with instructional materials like a blackboard, and possibly a video projector.

Safety and security.

Every school should have a security post, and security personnel that should go on parade from time to time. The safety of lives and property should be of paramount importance. The school authorities should endeavour to give talks about security consciousness to the students, and to staff as well. A very important facility that is good is the CCTV camera. Children may snick out of school, but the cameras would be able to tell when they left, and the probable exit route, and if they left with friends.

Parent Teacher Association (PTA)

PTAs provide a forum for the interaction of teachers and parents of the pupils. The school authorities should be open minded, allowing the parents to contribute to the development of various issues concerning the school, through suggestions and opinions. Parents on the other hand too should be open and participate actively in the affairs of the school. It is desirable to have a PTA in a standard school.

School accreditation.

Parents should verify the accreditation status of the school, if it is fully accredited or partially accredited. This fact can be confirmed from online sources, or from the Area Educational Office. Usually, a school that lacks accreditation is yet to have the standard requirements for starting a school. Some schools all over aren't accredited, though they continue with educational services illegally.

School reputation.

A school that has been in operation for a while should have a reputation in town. The school reputation consists of good and bad reputation, which has to do with major confirmed occurrences in the past, involving staff and students. This exposes the weakness and strengths in the system. A school where students have fought and inflicted injuries on one another on different occasions, not one, does not have a good reputation regarding safety of the students. Conversely, a school that is acclaimed to have had the best results in an external examination 5 consecutive times, has a good reputation.

CHAPTER 3

THE HOME ENVIRONMENT.

An appropriate home environment plays a great role in the academic development of a child. The home, fundamentally is the starting point for moral instructions, and all the important attributes that a child will then build upon outside the home. When there is a good and well organised home, there is always a potential for great success outside the home. It is often being said, that charity begins at home, and this statement cannot be overemphasised. Let's look at the attributes that every home should have for an excellent unlocking of a child's academic potentials.

There should be no family conflict.

The parents should ensure as much as possible to prevent friction and disagreements in the house, that may affect the child emotionally. This also affects decision making, because the parents tend to oppose one another. The child goes to school sad and moody, and most times unable to think straight in the class. The child may be confused, most times, because the disagreements are recurrent. Worse still is when there is a divorce, and there is no hope of the parents reconciling. Most children that are deviants have been shown to come from broken homes.

Supportive.

The home environment should be supportive, all the time. This support should not only be material, but emotional, as well. It is good for a child to be trained to work hard academically, but it is also more important for the child to passionately do this. In order words, the child has fallen in love with all learning g activities and shows motivation for same. A supportive environment actually stimulates the child to work hard and gives the child every good reason to work harder.

Routine.

There should be a routine to be followed in the home, which clearly shows the time to get up from bed daily, when to bathe, when to go to school, when to come back from school, when to study, and when to go to sleep. This leaves on a daily basis, the time to study. If this is not adhered to, many times, the study time could be used for other things, meaning that the child may not give time to study for days in a row. It also ensures that certain aspects of daily life are routinely observed, thereby making things less strenuous. The child is well organised and this gives a good propensity to do things excellently. It also teaches the child time management skills and maximal use of time.

Learning resources.

Though the home may really not be comparable to the school environment when it comes to learning, it should be able to have certain facilities, which aid learning at home. There should be a study area, and shouldn't be close to the dinning room or sitting room, because of distractions and noise. This study area should be well ventilated and should have a good set of ergonomically suited furniture. There should be adequate lighting as well. A blackboard, and markers are necessary. A good Internet connection is needed for the children to be able to access different resources on the Web.

Parental support.

Parents should be willing to lend extra support to their children that will serve as a source of motivation for these children and help them to push through challenges. Parents for instance on a daily basis willing to sit with the children and guide them through the home work, but not helping them to provide the answers. It is also necessary that a parent should try as much as possible to squeeze out time to attend school functions that require the presence of parents. One major aspect of parental obligation is to be able to engage the child in discussions in order to be able to get feedbacks as to how they fare at school.

Liberal atmosphere.

The home environment should be a Liberal atmosphere that gives the child a great opportunity to lean on the parents and be able to receive succour in times of challenges. There is no doubt that every child will be challenged at one time or the other. However, one good thing about it is the ability to be able to overcome the challenges, which is dependent upon having someone to share the problems with who would give an assurance that all will be well.

Role modelling.

Every parent should serve as a good example with regards to the things that they want the child to do or become. This is called role modelling. If you would like a child to take after the model of neat and smart dressing, then as a parent, you dress the same way always, for the child to copy you. If you would like the child to do some study after school for two hours, then you study or work on some assignment after work for three hours.

When you do these things, that is when the students follow after you.

Cross fertilisation of ideas.

Children should be allowed at home to play together, in as much as the association is a healthy one. This allows for cross fertilisation of ideas and talents. What is not being practised in school A is practiced in school B and vice-versa. Children should compare their experiences from one school to the other, and borrow some good ideas.

No favouritism.

As we consider a student individually at home, we need to look at a situation too, whereby there are many students at home. There should be no favouritism from one child to the other. Every child should be treated fairly. Every kid should get what they need without feeling that they are side-lined, or feeling discourage. Discouragement will bring about lack of motivation, which will affect academic performance, and by default, academic progress.

Comparisons.

When there are a number of students who live in the same home, there should be no comparisons, because every child is unique. In 2 Corinthians 10:12, the bible states "For we dare not make ourselves of the number, or compare ourselves with some that commend themselves: But they measuring themselves by themselves, and comparing themselves among themselves are not wise".

CHAPTER 4

GETTING TO KNOW YOUR CHILD

Every child has strengths, weaknesses, capabilities, gifts, and talents, that you need to discover, before you could unlock the true potentials of the child. The greatness of your child revolves around a knowledge of whom God says they are, that is, the innate and sterling qualities. According to Romans 8:30, every child was pre-destined, or assigned to carry out an assignment in life, and without discovering this, which they cannot manifest greatness.

The special abilities, gifts and talents refer to the divine purpose for which a child was created. The true potentials of a child lie in a merger of academic potentials and the unique abilities, and strengths. If a child tends to show interest for music, then as the days go by, it means that you need to channel the interest of the child to academic learning of the theory of music, side by side the performance or practical aspect. If a child shows a passion for caring for the sick, then you build academic learning directed at caring for the sick.

It is however good to note that demonstration of these qualities are dynamic to a point in life, and we need to track changes in interests and abilities as the child grows older. We eventually get to a point of no returns, that we can agree with all certainty that this is what a child is cut out to pursue in life. Celebrities worldwide were taught at an early stage to embrace their uniqueness and build on it. That is truly the secret to unlocking the true potentials of a child and manifesting of greatness!

The approach in this case is that once you discover the uniqueness of a child, you develop this by adding educational learning, and giving practical roles that align with this, creating opportunities for further self discovery and practicality. If there is any weakness observed, we try to instruct a child, or prepare them to overcome that weakness. A major weakness in most children is "fear", and it needs to be dealt with. Children should be instructed about how to develop faith, and positivity.

The truth is that the child spends more time at home than any other place, usually with the mothers. Mothers are in a better position to make the discovery, so that both parents can sit down and map out strategies to bring out the best in the child. The father too could observe and both husband and wife discuss their observations. If the ground work is concluded at home, and the discovery is made, then you could share with teachers that are in charge of their teaching or other activities for confirmation and implementation as appropriate.

Knowing who your child truly is may take a couple of years, but it is worth the patience, to make this discovery. Many potentials are wasted without discovering and developing these facts. They just lie dormant and waste away from cradle to grave. We shall now examine what it entails to truly discover who your child is, and what you need to know to make this discovery.

What are the factors to consider in determining the hidden potentials of a child?

Strong interests.

A child tends to have strong interests in certain activities which point to the type of gift or talent that they have. A child who is always there to care for the sick, whenever anybody is sick at home would do well in medical courses or social care. A child who likes to play puzzles would be good problem-solving skills and would do well in fields like Engineering. A child may however have more than these, but will always gravitate towards one.

Group dynamics.

It is worth noting the social preferences of a child, if they like to work in a group, or prefer to go solo. A child who prefers to work in a group has an affinity for collaborative work. This type of child will like activities that encourage group work, like discussion groups in class, or group projects or assignments. A child who likes to work independently will like more of individual work.

Such students prefer that they do it alone. A child who loves group work may be more active in group work, and do better in group work.

Learning style indices.

There are different kinds of learners, which include visual learners, auditory learners and kinesthetic learners. A visual learner responds more to visual aids, auditory learners respond more to things like story-telling, or listening to instructions, whilst kinesthetic learner. A kinesthetic learner does better in things that involve taking part in an activity. They like to participate in activities and do better in practical things. To bring out the best in each student, you must discover an indicator of your child's learning style.

Reaction to challenges.

Study the child's reaction to challenging situations. Does the child feel curious when faced with a challenge, or does the child feel frustrated when faced with a challenge? A child should be able to tolerate problems, adapt and overcome and not feeling overwhelmed. When a child is overwhelmed with challenges, such a trait indicates that the child needs to be taught to reverse this type of behaviour. Learning to tackle the bull by the horn, not getting frustrated brings out the best in a child.

Emotional expression.

The child should have how they communicate what they enjoy and what frustrates them. A child may communicate their emotions with drawing, another may communicate with singing, and yet another with story telling. All these activities may be used by a child to communicate their feelings, preferences and struggles. When the child is singing, then you try to draw a clue, or when the child is drawing.

Test instruments.

There are standardised questionnaires or instruments that could be used to assess the interests and preferences of a child formally or informally. When I say formal tests, I mean a standardised test, and research tested set of logical questions used to arrive at the interests and the nature of talents of a child, or their gifting. There are certain things you could assess without really sitting down to use a standardised instrument like reading fluency, writing skills, listening skills, memory skills and basic understanding. These could be assessed objectively or subjectively.

For older children who have the ability of understanding what they really love to do, you may ask them what are the things they love doing, the things they don't love doing at all, the things they find challenging, and the things they excel in. This method of self reflection helps them to understand their interrogative skills, and helps them to discover their strengths and abilities.

Collaborative efforts.

Parents, teachers and other professionals involved in the education of children need to collaborate, discuss and exchange opinions on what they think works best for the child. The teacher knows and discusses what happens at school, while the parents give their opinion about what happens at home. The Sunday school teacher may have a different view. All these views together should give a vivid impression about whom the child is.

Rotation of assignment.

When you rotate on assignments and observe, it is easy to know where the strengths and weaknesses are. Science experiments, furniture making, welding or cooking may reveal practical or kinesthetic strengths, while story telling and reading may point to a linguistic ability.

Review or adjustment.

Regular review or adjustment will reveal the strengths, weaknesses and preferences per time, because these parameters may change as the child grows up. Parents and teachers should be eager to assess and evaluate from time to time and work with the reality on ground.

Designing an educational program to build interest.

When the strengths, weaknesses and preferences are known, then it is necessary to draw a time-table and plan how to apply this knowledge, and build a program of studies aligned to the child's maximum potential. Things that constitute strengths that are in the child's life should be given an opportunity to manifest through activities. This also builds confidence as time goes on.

If a child is a visual learner, then you incorporate in his program a lot of videos and diagrams. A child like that would learn faster watching YouTube videos. He or she would also like reading books or material with a lot of diagrams. A kinesthetic learner would prefer practical subjects, or things that are participatory. These ones would enjoy using games for example to simulate real life situations.

Leadership tendencies.

There are children that not only like to work in groups, they have social strength, and also like showing leadership tendencies. Once this is noted, you give them leadership roles as a team leader, assistant team leader, or roles in representative capacity.

Overcoming weaknesses.

Simplify challenges.

A child whose weakness is in reading could be helped with audio books. Another approach is "paired reading". In paired reading, two people read together. One of them is a slow reader, whilst the other is fast. It helps build fluency and confidence on the part of the slower reader. A good example of paired reading may be between a child and his mother or father, or between a child and his teacher. The fast reader could ask questions to test comprehension.

Multi-sensory approach.

The multi-sensory approach leverages on using the operations of multiple senses, where one sense is deficient. If for example a child struggles with hearing, then with this approach, you incorporate more visual activities, or reinforce with visual activities or hands-on activities.

Encourage persistence.

The aim of this is that the child should not be allowed to give up or lose interest in seemingly difficult activities. The approach is to break down the activities into smaller tasks, and set achievable goals. Then celebrate small achievements to encourage the child and keep them motivated for resilience and a growth mind-set.

Adapting learning preferences.

In this, you make the learning environment suitable to the child's learning style. This means that the difficult subjects or areas of his or her weakness should be taught using videos or games, if he or she prefers to learn watching videos.

Introduce variety to learning.

Make available a variety of learning resources and note which area the student prefers. Then you may tend to repeat the use of this learning method that the student prefers. In this way, they get assimilate more. Flexibility in learning is the key word here as you incorporate choice even within a task. The learning process is broken down that they find it very easy.

Real-life applications.

Real life applications can be very interesting and stimulating. If a child has problems with fractions and decimals, then you may want to take them through a cooking class. They measure palm oil, salt, water and other ingredients in fractions, that you may even tell them to do some calculations. After cooking, you may also give them proportions as to how to share the food. This makes them understand easily and very interesting.

Developing social strength.

In order to Foster social skills, children that love socialising could be brought together to learn in participatory and group activities for them to develop their skills in team work further. The ones that specifically love leadership should be appointed to play leadership roles in the groups, and the teacher or parent stimulates such a child to give feedback.

Building emotional regulation.

Children should be taught to understand, express and manage their emotions. The parent or teacher should model emotions with the appropriate vocabulary. A sentence like I feel happy because my husband just got me a new car. Or a sentence like I feel sad because I just lost a sizeable amount of money. Give them the opportunity to express their emotions freely, making them to know that it is good to embrace emotions. Let them partake in activities that help to manage their emotions like drawing, painting, singing and dancing.

CHAPTER 5

MOTIVATION

What is motivation?

Motivation is the internal or external instinct that stimulates and directs behaviour for the purpose of achieving a goal. Motivating children for academics is a broad approach that gives recognition to their psychological, emotional, and intellectual needs.

Three major elements are important in motivation. The first is

Activation: The decision to start a behaviour, task or project is known as activation.

Persistence: the act of sustaining the effort involved to achieve the goal

Intensity: The level of attention and energy directed towards achieving a goal.

Sources of motivation.

Motivation can arise from the child's perception, thoughts and beliefs. Things that make a child happy would generally cause a motivation. This is known as intrinsic motivation.

The second type of motivation is known as extrinsic motivation. This arises from things that are seen or experienced. Prizes, certificates, or small prizes as short-term rewards are good examples. This value of things may change from time to time as the child grows.

Setting goals.

In order for children to be motivated there should be mapped out goals which should not only be clear, but attainable and give a sense of direction and achievement. The tasks should be graded from less challenging to more challenging ones.

Positive environment.

A learning environment that is positive is appealing to the senses and could motivate a student to learn, thereby bringing the best academic potentials in the child. The environment should be free of forms of bitterness, toxicity and resentment, with the child being able to express himself or herself readily. Positive reinforcements should be directed towards the effort put into study and not the results of the academic pursuits.

Promoting a growth mind-set.

Children should be taught that challenges are not meant to break them, but to strengthen them. They should be told to note the importance of persevering and working hard through challenges.

Learning strategy.

A good Learning strategy should be developed depending on the peculiarities of the child. Ideally a child that loves videos should be thought using videos. Real life situations as much as possible should incorporated into the syllabus of the subject. Allow flexibility and thinking outside the box.

A good rapport.

Parents should care for their children and believe in them, and likewise teachers should care for their students too. When children see that you are confident about them they feel happy and are motivated to perform better. Exchange ideas with them, and speak with them.

Feedbacks.

Every child is anxious to receive a feedback from the teachers or parents. This encourages them to work harder if they do well. However, while being positive and enthusiastic, the truth about their situation needs to be told them but in a loving way. Celebrate small wins.

Self assessment skills.

Every child should be thought to be responsible. One of the major routes to being responsible is self assessment. They should be able to manage time and resources efficiently. This fosters a sense of responsibility and accountability.

Take away pressure.

Children do not like been pressurised and love to be understood. If you are not patient, it is impossible to draw out the best in them. There is always a need to take away pressure, because they are naturally responsibve

CHAPTER 6

GIFTS AND TALENTS

One cannot fully unlock the potentials of a child without discovering and developing the natural gifts and talents. When a gift is natural, you are born with it, and it is a divine endowment. It is not without a reason, that God has given that special ability. The true greatness of a child lies in them identifying and using their gifts. It is the gift of God in a child that makes him or her a celebrity, and a world figure, for example music.

The great thing about a gift is that everyone on the surface of the earth has at least, one gift. Every child born into the world has been given a key to open doors. This is the gift of God upon your life. It is the responsibility of the parents at the very early stages in life to help the child to discover this gift(s). There are children as well that discover these gifts by themselves, later in life. It is surprising however that many people have an ability that they are unaware of. I never knew I could be good on guitar until it was revealed to me by God.

There are things to note about a gift.

The gift of God in a child is that thing that the child is passionate about doing, and loves doing.

The gift of God is that thing that a child does without much effort or struggle.

The gift of God in your life is that thing that you do excellently well.

The gift of God in a child's life is what distinguishes him or her amongst the crowd.

The gift of God attracts favour to your life with men and angels.

The gift of God naturally attracts blessings to a person's life.

In spite of all these advantages, many parents ignore the gifts of God in their children, identify their children as whom they are not, and call them the name that God has not given to them. Whenever man decides to side track God's design and plan for a child, he would only meet with a hard wall!

There are children, who are uncomfortable with their "man made vocations", and eventually discover their purpose and pursue it passionately. If the gift of God is so strong upon a life, but the person does not pursue it, it may bring dissonance, lack of fulfilment and sorrow. This is why it is desirable to take into cognisance the gift of a child. The truth is that there is something unique about your child, and you need to discover that uniqueness. It is the secret of the child's rising and shinning. The world is waiting for the uniqueness in your child to manifest gloriously. That gift is waiting to be blessed across the world. Discover it now!

How to discover the gifts and uniqueness in a child.

By observation.

When you observe a child over time, you would begin to discover a pattern regarding those things that the child is excited about doing. A child may like to sing and hum, all the time. A child may like acting with the neighbour's children and sometimes ignore food or other things. That type of child is an actor, or actress.

Then you should observe the things that this child loves doing. Another thing is that there are some abilities that manifest naturally. Some children at a very early stage manifest the prophetic gift, and when they say something, it comes to pass. Children like that should be encouraged. Also pay attention to those things they like discussing or their perceived role models.

Exposure to variety.

A parent may not know that a child has an interest in a particular activity, or are gifted in it, or enjoy it, until they are exposed to it. A child might not develop an interest in snookers or billiards, until they are exposed to it per chance in a club. Let them have a go. There is always a hidden treasure in a child that you must help them to dig and bring out to shine. Encourage extracurricular activities at home, in the school, and outside of home or school, for example in clubs.

Encourage creativity.

Children should be given the opportunity to explore things outside the conventional ideas. They should attempt to do things their own way. They might listen to a song, but you tell them to try and sing it in another way, sometimes you may give examples, or initiate it, taking the lead. There are children with exceptional gifts that unless you encourage creativity, it won't manifest. A child may dance in a unique way, that no one can do. He may whistle to produce music in a special way.

A conducive environment.

This an environment that truly and wholly supports the interests and ambitions of the child which allows him or her to work unhindered. It is an environment that encourages the child, and supports the child in every possible way, to manifest the gift for all to see. A child with a musical gift would most probably manifest fully the gift for example where there is a keyboard to play.

In this type of environment, he or she also has people that practice the same thing or have the same inclinations.

Facilitate their ambitions.

There are gifts that require facilitation in terms of providing the required instruments. A child who is interested in drawing and painting needs poster paints, oil paints, paint brushes, soft pencils, and others. A child who is interested in singing and playing an instrument would need the particular instrument for example a saxophone, and other associated musical instruments. Specialist trainings and examinations might be necessary as well, on a regular basis, which should be provided for.

Goal setting.

Break down the tasks, and help them to set goals. A child who is learning to play a musical instrument needs musical theory. Help them to break down the music theory grades and you may say a grade per month, and make sure they achieve it. The songs to play are also categorised into different categories, setting goals and attaching a time that it should be completed.

Mentorship.

The best person to be able to help a child after sometime is a mentor or coach. If a child is interested in Fine Arts, a Fine Arts teacher or an artist would be in a good position to help the child where there are challenges. This is because they have passed through the same stage. If a child is interested in Music, a Music teacher or musician is in a good position to help the child to develop the gift.

Allow some autonomy.

A child should sometimes be able to decide for themselves what they want or they feel like doing, even as they exercise their gifts. Sometimes as well, they might be bored, as everything might be monotonous. Try and allow them to do something they feel like doing. A child who likes drawing may prefer to do textiles now, which is fine. A child who sings may love to try an instrument. There should be autonomy and flexibility so that the child can discover the best potential that they have.

Prayer.

Prayer has a great role to play in discovering and developing the abilities, gifts and talents of a child. The Bible says in Romans 8:30, that as many as he did predestinate, them he called: and whom he called, them he also justified: and whom he justified, them he also glorified. God has a plan for every destiny, and because of this, he planted gifts. He knows us from our mother's wombs and it is from him we could get the original plan. This includes the gift. Every parent should pray and fast continuously to discover the plan of God for the child on earth. If parents tarry in prayer, God tells what the gift of the child is, where he should use it, the people the child is sent to, the dos and don't. Divine information about a child's gift is usually very accurate.

The case study of Albert Einstein.

Albert was a German Physicist that lived between 1879 to 1955. He was born in Ulm, Germany, and as a child showed an interest in science and mathematics, as a student in Munich, Germany, in his early childhood years. He eventually relocated with his parents and ended up studying Physics and Mathematics at the Polytechnic Institute in Zurich, Switzerland.

History had it that Albert was a late talker, who was only able to talk at the age of 4 years old. This is suggestive that he was developmentally delayed. Though he showed interest in Physics and Mathematics, he was challenged educationally that his teachers complained about him as being a difficult and rebellious and added that he wouldn't become much in life. The situation was that bad.

However, his teachers were not patient enough to observe him enough to discover his natural interests in Mathematics and Physics. As at that time, generally in Germany, the educational system was very rigid and strict, that parents and teachers were more interested in the overall performance of the child.

Albert was interested in numerate disciplines and was not that good in literature, history, poetry and the likes. The challenge even was more due to his late talking. When the challenge was much, his parents changed his school to another school in Munich. Somewhere along the line, the parents relocated to Italy, for work while he remained in Germany. His results were still not looking good enough as he left Germany without certificate to show his for his work. He had left with a medical certificate, without the successful completion of his course of studies.

Albert had to join his parents in Italy, but he had to undergo a period of independent studies during which he studied his Mathematics and Physics at an in-depth, according to what he learnt initially. This formed the ground work for all that he did in later years. He had to relocate to Zurich in Switzerland, where he had access to a more progressive and supportive education.

Characteristics of a progressive style of education.

It engages curiosity.

The children are exposed to a variety of activities that are involved in different types of vocation and profession. The children over time develop a curiosity and an interest towards certain activities. Once this happens, the student is supported and engaged in such an activity. It might take time for such an interest to be detected but it is worth the waiting.

Real-world projects and practical applications.

Students are taken to factories or work sites, depending on their interests. A child who is interested in electronics is posted to an electronic equipment manufacturing company, and exposed to the practical applications. This further stimulates interest, and engages the student further.

Independent thinking.

Complex problems are introduced at the level of the student to stimulate individual thinking. As the students attempt to solve the problems, they brainstorm and study harder to provide solutions. The result is that these students gradually evolve and are able to solve more complex problems.

Promotes group activities and team work.

Group activities theoretically and practically help to foster team work, and for students to learn to accept and respect the views others in their team. At times, they team together to write an essay, or they might team together to make a craft item. When students work with peers, there is excitement and confidence. Children tend to be more resilient when they work together, as well as being more creative. Inclusivity is another advantage that is derived when children work together in a group.

Focus on the whole child.

In education, a focus on the academic abilities or academic progress wouldn't bring out the best in a child. Of great importance is the emotional aspects, social interactions and ethical development. Every teacher should be interested in the emotions of a child, as they are being taught, so that they can be impacted maximally. An angry child or sad child may not be effectively taught except the underlying issue is addressed. When the social interaction is poor, and the child does not relate with other people, it is a problem.

Flexibility.

Learning styles should be flexible, and sometimes the learning times. In Lagos, Nigeria at a time, we had morning classes, as well as afternoon classes. Many people welcomed the afternoon classes, and there was a massive enrolment. This is an example of the concept of flexibility. For students that enjoy viewing, videos could be employed in learning, and not only writing on the chalk board.

Furthermore, in contemporary times, there are lots of challenges, and societal problems, yet, students must be instructed. The Covid-19 example is a vivid one. People soon got used to studying online. This is a good example of flexible learning. Well into 2022, for example, many university students were in Africa, and receiving lectures steadily in the United Kingdom. Education should take cognisance of the individual, group, and societal needs at a particular point in time.

Preparation for life.

Every student should be taught skills that are applicable beyond school, and useful in everyday life. Communication, creativity, empathy and adaptability are all skills that should be taught, which the students will use for life.

CHAPTER 7

DISCIPLINE

Discipline in education is making students obey rules, regulations, or standards of behaviour, and imposing punishments when same are not obeyed. It is necessary for personal development and success in life. Discipline fosters self control, responsibility, social conformity, and the ability to be able to focus on the important things which will later make then responsible and successful adults.

Without discipline, no great achievements are possible. A child therefore must be disciplined if their best potential must be achieved. An undisciplined child would eventually have problems manifesting the greatest academic potentials they are capable of. This begins from being able to wake up early enough in the day to prepare for school, and ensuring they get to school punctually. In this case, the parent too has a role to play by serving as a role model. If the parents are not disciplined then it would affect the child.

Discipline is involved also in how the child engages in class. This is partly a responsibility of the class teacher to ensure that the child pays attention in class, by not doing other things when the lessons are going on. Enthusiasm in the activities in the class also requires discipline, and ensuring participation. If there are any deadlines for assignments, then they should be met. Home work should be done properly. It is the responsibility of the parents to ensure that assignments are done. This is part of discipline too.

Good social etiquette should be adhered to, in the relationship between the child and the colleagues. The manner of relationship with others in the society and what the child could do in the society are all dependent on discipline. Discipline shapes the character of a child, and also the destiny. It is about knowing what to do and what not to do in a particular place, at a particular time. Discipline created a good foundation for the destiny of the child.

This is one of the advantages of boarding schools. In a boarding school, there is strict adherence to laid down rules, without which punishments may be imposed. Children who attend boarding schools are highly disciplined, but sometimes, in a few schools, the treatment may be too harsh, as care takers may be inconsiderate or harsh. These untoward tendencies need to be addressed for the experience of the child in the boarding school to be worthwhile.

Barriers to effective discipline in children.

Poor role modelling.

Children copy from role models, and in these formative years of their lives, the examples they draw from the role models has long lasting effects upon their lives. A role model includes a parent, a teacher, or a carer. A role model has to know the truth, teach them the truth, and be consistent with following the truth. Any consistency lapses will confuse the child. If for example, you taught the child to wake up by 6 a.m., but as a role model, you wake up at 6.45 a.m. or 7 a.m. or even later, this will affect the level of discipline in the child. A role model needs to do the right things and be consistent in doing them.

Lack of role model collaboration.

The school instils a lot of discipline in the child, based on the instructions and activities they perform. However, if a child gets home and the same standards are unobtainable, then this leads to lapses and unseriousness for the child. The child may even tend to disregard the school rules, thinking that the lifestyle at home is the better. This creates a conflict in the mind of the child which might lead to indiscipline.

Too mean or too lenient discipline.

The rules and regulations have to be realistic, and punishment should not be too overwhelming. If a child wakes up at 4 a. m. that is a bit harsh. Also, if a child is allowed to wake up late because you try to justify it, then it would be too lenient. Too strict discipline could lead to fear, resentment, and rebellion. Overly lenient discipline would eventually be lack of discipline, and the results are unachievable. The key word is optimism. Not too harsh and not too lenient. A set of rules could be adjusted gradually to make them realistic.

Mental health issues.

Children with mental health issues, autism, cerebral palsy and similar conditions may find it difficult adhering to rules always, and may struggle with meeting up expectations. This category of students needs a lot of support or a tailored approach. Good enough, some of them adapt and are able to cope, if the parents or teachers continue without any lapses.

Lack of structure and routine.

There should be an established routine or time table that the student should use at home or at school. When there is a time table, the student knows what to do at a particular time, and which failure to do it attracts a punishment. Routines help children to build expectations and understand consequences. There should be an established structure at home and at school. The student spends more time at home, including the weekends, and parents should not be lackadaisical about enforcing a sound routine at home.

Association.

Any association with negative or unserious people would make it difficult to be disciplined. This is especially true for adults who are in care capacity, or peers. Indiscipline can negatively influence the perception of a child as to a proper behaviour. Parents should be cautious about the type of company their children keep at home. This mindset would also follow the child to school, because teachers may not have time for that apart from core academic matters.

How to instil discipline in children.

Have a time table.

When there is a time table, the expected routine is clear. There is also an awareness that there are punishments attached to non-adherence. This will motivate the child to behave properly and stick with the regulations. In as much as this routine is consistently followed, compliance becomes automatic, and discipline is ensured.

Balance in activities.

There should be a balanced structure of activities like academics, recreational activities and breaks. If there is no balance, the time table may be monotonous and not practicable. However, if the timetable is well structured, then there could be no monotony then balance and discipline can be achieved in the real sense.

Excellent role modelling.

If there are defects in the attitude and behaviour of role models, it would reflect in the behaviour of the child. In the school environment, the teachers and other carers are the role models, while at home, the parents and other people who take care of the children are the role models. Role modelling should be highly intentional.

Engaged learning.

Children should be engaged in their learning, by involving then in academic schedules to some extent. If they are pre-informed before involvement, there is less likelihood towards rebellion or indiscipline.

Time management.

An important area of daily life, where discipline is reflected is time management. When there is no discipline, time would not be well managed, with resultant effects on the potentials of the child. The children should be taught how to prioritise, and apportion time to each activity in a way to make the best out of their day, their week, and their term.

Feedbacks.

It is a good thing and the responsibility of teachers to provide feedbacks on the performance of the child. When a child is given feedbacks on their activities, then they can caution themselves and be disciplined. The reason for providing feedbacks in this case, is that the child should conform to expected norms. Objectives of the different activities should be well communicated to every child.

Set realistic goals.

Frustration and demotivation could set in, if the goals set by parents or teachers are unattainable by the child. A good approach as earlier stated is to break down the activities to make them achievable per time or otherwise, so that the children find it easy. This way, there is no frustration and demotivation.

Reflections on approach.

The child should be made to reflect on how they have approached issues, and the results they had. Therefore, it is not just about the results achieved academically, buy the approach too needs to be evaluated, so that the children would be able to know where they have gone wrong and revise the approach, and be able to do things differently, and better. This facilitates orderliness and discipline.

CHAPTER 8

OVERCOMING CHALLENGES IN CHILDREN

An educational challenge is a difficulty or hindrance that negatively affects the ability to teach, learn or allow the academic potentials of a child to be maximised. These challenges could originate from teachers, students or the educational system. Generally, they could be as a result of personal, social, or structural factors. In order to maximise the academic potentials in a child, these challenges need to be tackled by teachers and parents. A collaborative approach is most beneficial, and we thank God that this is possible.

Types of educational challenges

Learning disabilities.

Learning disabilities are impairments of function that make a child unable to process information or coordinate movements or activities important in learning. These disabilities are usually inherited, associated with a pathology of the brain, and may also be due to environmental factors like exposure to toxins or even medications and alcohol. This includes dyslexia, which causes difficulties with word recognition, decoding, and spelling, slow reading speed, problems with reading comprehension. Dyscalculia is another one, which causes difficulty in grasping number concepts, learning mathematics, performing calculations, and related problems.

Dysgraphia is another Learning disability which causes a defective writing ability, including the physical act of writing and the understanding of written items. There are difficulties with spelling and sentence structure. Auditory processing disorder impacts how the brain processes spoken language, difficulty differentiating between similar sounds, problems with following instructions, as well as difficulty in learning in noisy environments. Children with this condition usually don't do well in long discussions.

Visual processing disorder is another learning disability that affects the ability to interpret visual information, including problems with reading, and interpretation of charts, graphs and associated materials. In Non-Verbal Learning Disability (NVLD), this affects interpretation of body languages, facial expressions and other non-verbal cues. A student with this condition may struggle with understanding social situations or organising physical space.

Resource problems.

Educational materials, such as textbooks, exercise books, pencils, pens, erasers, mathematical sets and other materials should be made available. Likewise, audio-visual materials, and sports equipment should be made available. Human resources also constitute an important aspect when it comes to maximising educational potentials in children. Parents should make it a point of duty to provide adequately for their children.

Socioeconomic barriers.

Finance has a big role in the choice of education available to a child, as well as the ability to be able to provide for the necessary needs of the child. Another related issue is access to the education due to social impediments. Majority of children who are unable to attend school and maximise their academic potentials come from financially disadvantaged homes. There is a substantial role that finance has to play. If the social infrastructure like libraries, community development programs relating to education are not there, there would be problems.

Language barriers.

The child must be proficient in the language of instruction of the school being attended. The child should also be proficient in the language of the community. Both the language of the school and community affect the education of the child, especially the language of instruction in the school being attended by the child. Even if a child is intelligent, but is in a foreign land that the child does not understand the language, there would be learning problems and the child cannot manifest the best potential. This is true for a child relocating to Germany into a school that the language of instruction is German, and vice-versa.

Emotional problems.

The emotional health of a child must be well guarded to ensure concentration and excellent performance in the class. A child who is always depressed, or who has anxiety issues due to ill-treatment at home cannot be at his best in school. Marital problems in the child's family, especially children from broken homes tend to affect them emotionally and reflecting in their academic performance.

Physical disabilities.

Physical disabilities can be so emotionally devastating to a child that it affects the performance at school. This needs a lot of support and encouragement, for the child to be able to concentrate at school. There is always a tendency to lack of self worth, or low self esteem which affects academic pursuits. Consider the need for wheel chair or writing gadgets, and how readily they may be available. A physical disability can be very children.

Differences in culture.

Communication differences might affect learning in some climes. A student who was born and raised in Nigeria wouldn't possibly be outspoken when she is in the UK and Canada, even though she is more intelligent than everyone, except she adapts to that culture. This would limit her potentials. Likewise, a child who comes from a religious background where they have extended fasting annually may be affected during these fasts. Also, in countries where there is time consciousness live.

Overcrowded classrooms.

When the ratio of Teacher to Student is too high, then we say that the classroom is overcrowded. The optimal teacher-student ratio depends on factors like the average age of the children, subject matter, like subjects that entail practical demonstrations, teaching methods, and socio-economic background where students may need individualised attention. In the nursery school, the number of students to a teacher should not be more than fifteen, and in the primary school, twenty, and earlier years of secondary school, twenty-five.

Curriculum defects.

The curriculum may pose challenges against the ability to be able to bring out the best potentials in a child. The curriculum should follow after a specific requirement by the education authorities. However, some schools use a deficient curriculum lacking in a few subjects, or might be too rigid. Curricula should be flexible even though within the overall frame work to address the individual needs of a student.

How to address educational challenges.

Teacher training.

Excellent teacher training is important, because the teachers can't give what they don't have, nor pour from an empty cup. Basically, the teachers should have good entry qualifications and should have studied their courses as majors in education. An engineering graduate teaching physics or mathematics would not produce the best results.

Another thing is to employ teachers who are not just specialised, but experienced for example in learning disabilities. These teachers should also impact other teachers with their wealth of knowledge.

Early identification.

It is always better to identify educational challenges early so that they could be handled early. Overcoming educational challenge may take time, so it's pretty better to start on time, especially learning disabilities or emotional problems. It starts with screening before therapy. In the school setting, authorities should take interest in carrying out periodical screening of the students to discover these things.

Targeted programs.

At its best, targeted programs should be tailored towards addressing specific needs in children. Teachers should outline the goals, and map out the strategies towards meeting the goals and objectives. This type of program brings about quick progress and could be administered while the student is part of the larger class. This is one of the advantages of smaller classes as targeted and individualised programs are possible. This will help the eventual result of the student.

Parent-Teacher Cooperation.

Overcoming educational challenges can never be unilateral, but bilateral. The first reason is that the child stays both at home and at school, and stakeholders are responsible on either side. There has to be mutual cooperation. The second issue lies in the fact that the parents provide for the needs of the child and couldn't be excluded from the overall picture. The results are wonderful if the parent-teacher understanding and cooperation is strong.

Variety of learning methods.

Students belong to different learning categories like visual, auditory and kinesthetic learners. In order to overcome academic challenges, teachers need to identify which group each child belongs, and is better suited to their needs. If you are teaching elementary science for example, some are happy to listen to you teach, some like to watch the video, whilst some will like to plant the bean seed in a can and watch how it grows.

Technology.

Education and academic performance could receive a boost by means of different types of information technology interventions. These make learning more stimulating and interesting, especially for children. There are platforms that help manage subjects and track progress, as well as a variety of apps to teach specific skills and subjects especially the languages.

There is video conferencing whereby students in different school could study together and exchange views. There are assisting technology for students with audio-visual impairment like "speech to text" and specialised computer keyboards.

Positive reinforcements.

In this method, the parent or teacher observes the areas that the student performs best. They praise the child each time he does well, and encourage him the more. This builds confidence and further hard work and motivation in the life of the child.

Scholarship and financial aid.

Lack of financial resources often may constitute a challenge with regards to the education of a child. Schools and government agencies have financial assistance which could be available based on need or expression of interest. This limits the problems of the child and can allow them to make progress in their education.

Prayer.

Prayer is the best type of activity you could possibly engage in in order to overcome challenges in the life of a child. The Holy Spirit through prayer reveals to you, the problems of the child through Prayer, and what needs to be done to overcome it. Through Prayer, God mobilises spiritual resources, and angelic intervention to help your child. It is however that the understanding of the modern man is so darkened that many despise the importance of prayer. Prayer gives revelation, which is the key that unlocks every potential.

CHAPTER 9

UNRAVELLING THE EXAMINATION PARADOX

Examinations have been depended upon throughout history, as an evaluative tool for student achievement. However, we are aware that sometimes, an examination instrument (exam questions) may be invalid, and very unreliable. In most cases, the exam questions are tested with mock students, and the instrument examined for errors, before finally using it and setting as an examination. Yet there mat still be errors.

In other words, a student may be very brilliant, and not perform as the average student in class. Here lies the paradox and mystery of an examination. So, sometimes, the performance of a child cannot be said to quantify the achievement of the student. To this end, the student should learn strategies about how to pass an exam.

The result in the examination is what would be used to judge the elevation to another level, and whether the result truly represents student ability may not really matter. Students therefore should strategically prepare for examinations.

What are the facts to note about passing an examination?

Preparation.

One of the things to note is that excellence in an exam is the product of good preparation. Right from the beginning of the term, a study schedule should be drawn and followed. One good practice is that unfailingly and consistently, on a daily basis, every subject that is taught at school must be revised thoroughly again, and the child should be tested on the things so learnt with various methods. Try and include practical sessions as much as possible to rule out monotony.

Treat past examination questions.

This is a very important aspect of examination preparation. There are past examination questions that are kept by the school. There are also External examination questions that could be bought, in many countries of the world. Each time a child studies, then relevant questions from the exam questions are solved with him or her, and scored, and corrections made.

Marking scheme.

Just practicing with past questions is not enough, if you have not been able to see and familiarise yourself with the marking scheme. In the marking scheme, students may be required to write answers to two decimal places. If a student doesn't know this, they will score low marks.

There are also steps that need to be followed very clearly in solving a sum in Arithmetic. This should be practices with the child, making sure he is familiar with it.

Good nutrition.

The brain of the child, as well as the body systems require good nutrition to function well and write and pass exams. The diets should not only be balanced, but timely too. Mind you, children should not be overfed in such a way that they don't want to have so much interest in studying.

Time management skills.

A major reason that makes students to fail in exams is lack of proper time management. The child to be made to solve the questions under exam conditions, including time. However, also let them know that easier questions should first be attempted and solved.

Conducive environment.

To get the maximum assimilation during study, the environment must be very quiet without distractions. There should be ear pieces for video viewing. The furniture should be very comfortable and the study area shouldn't be close to the kitchen. Efforts should be made to ensure that there are not too many students to cause noise making, though peer interaction has it's own advantages.

Peer learning.

Students are able to relate with one another with ease, when they are in the midst of people of the same age group. Where possible, that should be encouraged. There are areas in the curriculum, where one of the students may have discovered as interesting. The way he or she presents it, they enthusiastically accept it. Group or peer learning is good, but the purpose should not be abused or the attention diverted.

Final revision.

At about two weeks to the examination, when the timetable is out, then there should be a revision of all the studies for the term. Most schools revise the terms work with their students, but it is apt for parents to draw a revision time table at home too, based on the work for the term Run through all the theory and practical aspects of things thought in the term.

CHAPTER 10

WHEN YOU LET GOD TAKE CONTROL.

God is our creator, the Almighty, who is everywhere, knows all things, and can do all things. Every child that is in this world has been assigned with abilities, and given a great assignment, with a great destiny. If this specific assignment is not discovered, then the child may be likened to a man building on another man's plot, or a person running in the wrong direction with all his strength. It would always be an exercise in futility and frustration.

There are specific gifts that a child is endowed with by God to use on their journey on earth (Isaiah 43:7). However, if a parent shows preferences for a particular occupation or profession, and wants the child to pursue that, that kind of child would end up being frustrated in life. In the first place, he might take several years to gain admission to study that course, and even when the child has graduated, he doesn't have an interest, nor the human endowment to succeed in that occupation.

The result is that a child cannot be the best, where God has not assigned him. In this case, many children's destinies have been diverted and frustrated due to bad parenting. One great heritage that a child can have from the parents is a knowledge of whom they are. They need to be taught and follow the plan of God with great focus. In Jeremiah 29:11 (NIV), God says, I know the plans that I have for you, plans to prosper you and not to harm you to give you a hope and a future.

The plans of a bright and glorious future in a child has already been decided and planned by God, and no parent should tamper with it. In Romans 8:30, the bible says as many as he did predestinate, them he called, as many as he called, then he justified, and as many as he justified, them he glorified. This means that the success of a child depends on a knowledge of predestination and who God says he is from the foundation of the world.

A child cannot fulfil destiny and be greater than his heavenly identity and purpose, because God knows far much more than we can ever think or imagine. There are three main things we need for a child to be at his or her best and maximise potential in thus world. The first thing is that he needs to have spirit filled parents that would lead him in the journey to discover his destiny, and secondly there has to be a knowledge of who the child is by prayer and revelation. The third one is that the child also needs to be spirit filled, in order to align with God's will, and fulfil destiny. A spirit filled child would always crave doing scriptural things always, and be divinely ordered in his or her preferences.

Revelation of predestination.

God has endowed every child a gift that would be needed in their life's journey. It is the responsibility of "both" parents and not just one parent to collaborate and discover whom their child is, and agree to help the child to become whom God says he is. There are many ways to do this as we have discussed earlier in Chapter five of this book. Parents should regularly put before God to reveal to them who their children are. This should be done with prayer and fasting. Teachers also have a role to play.

I do not just want to believe that everyone reading this book is a Christian. When I say Christian, I mean that you have confessed Jesus Christ as your Lord and personal saviour. The Bible says, in Romans 10:10 that with the heart, man believeth unto righteousness; and with the mouth, confession is made unto salvation. The most important thing to start with as a parent, or as a child who is able to comprehend what it means to surrender their lives to Jesus, if they have not yet done so.

Say this: Lord Jesus, I thank you because you are my saviour, and you laid down your life for me, on the cross of Calvary. I confess you as Lord and saviour over my life today, and I reject the devil and all his evil works. Thank you, Lord Jesus, for all that you did for me. Amen.

The next thing is for you to forsake your sin. In James 4:17, the bible says that to him that knoweth to do good, and doeth it not, it is sin. The Bible also says in Romans 14:23, that he who doubts is condemned if he eats, because he eateth not of faith. Anything you do of a doubtful heart is sin, and by implication, not to take care of your children or provide for them, if it erodes your conscience, it is sin. The conscience would always convict of sin, and it is important to always listen to our conscience. Anything sinful is outside God's will, and you need to do away with such to enjoy God's plans and promises.

It is by confessing positively what the word of God says, meditating in the word of God, and practicing the word of God that brings about success. The word of God is a "safeguard", so to say, against every negative tendency. The parents and children should follow God's word. However, it is good to separate the duties of a spirit filled child and that of spirit filled parents in maximising potentials in a child.

The spirit filled parent.

The spirit filled parent basically must have confessed Jesus Christ and surrendered themselves completely to Jesus. This has to be the mum and dad of the child. They also need to have forsaken sin and should be willing to run away from anything sinful that is not in God's will. They should also belong to a church, and make sure that their child is enrolled in the children church. The roles of a spirit filled parent are as follows;

Teach the child morals and discipline.

Morals and discipline help to channel the interests and desires of a child to align with expected behaviour. Parents should make sure that the children follow bible teachings and morals. The child should always be reminded to study. It is also good for parents to help develop certain qualities in their children like how to keep money. When to study, and how they could study.

Word study.

Parents owe the responsibility of initiating and leading them through bible study, be it by reading or by television or videos, drawing their attention to insights for daily living. The main purpose of studying at this stage is to draw the attention of children to truths that will strengthen their beliefs and behaviour. It is also expected that through word study, they should be able to deal with life's challenges more readily.

Pray with the children.

Praying with the children helps them to cultivate the habit of praying at the right times, and teaching them what to pray about. Gradually they should be taught how to fast. Once you tell a child that prayers are potent and works wonders, and by showing them relevant parts of the scripture, they believe you.

Discover gifts and talents.

It is the responsibility of parents to observe their kids, and prayerfully discover their gifts. This may not be something that would happen in a few weeks, but may take up to 2 or more years. The gifts of a child could be dynamic, and change with time, and the parents over time should be able to say categorically on the overall assessment, who a child is, especially when combined with prayer. When a parent prays and, in the dream, they see their child as a Baker, dressed in a white apron, they just got to accept it, and not try to change it.

Defence of the child.

Sometimes, a child may be in a helpless situation where they have been abused or relegated. A parent must be able to defend the child, and sometimes may need to visit their school, if attention is needed. Meetings like the parents-teachers association meeting should be attended by parents. All these supports give a child a sense of belonging and confidence in themselves, which helps them to stand strong in challenging times.

Dream journaling and spiritual sensitivity.

In 1 Samuel 3:1, the bible tells us that and the *child* Samuel ministered unto the Lord before Eli. The Bible confirms further in Acts 2:17, God says that in the last days, I will pour out my spirit upon all flesh, and your sons and your daughters shall prophesy, and your young men shall see visions, and your old men shall dream dreams. In Joel 2:28, this is reiterated.

Children usually have a propensity to have revelations, probably because their minds are not clogged with worries and anxieties like adults. Some children are really gifted and catch very clear revelations. It is therefore the responsibility of a parent to sensitize them to dreams and visions, and to make sure that they keep a journal or exercise book to record and keep the records of these revelations. Parents should take them to the Pastor or other spiritual mentors, and make sure they learn to live their lives based on these revelations.

Receiving and giving feedbacks.

All children have some things to say based on their relationships with parents. These are called feedbacks which they share with parents. Parents on the other hand do also give backs to their children on how they feel about their activities and impact those activities may have on their lives. Parents give feedbacks to the children and children give feedbacks to parents in a cyclic fashion. These feedbacks help to regulate and stabilise the attitude and behaviour of the children, which is called discipline.

Types of revelation.

Like we have seen above, it is the ordination of God for children to have revelations, and many children have revelational gifts (1 Corinthians 12) like the gifts of words of wisdom, words of knowledge, prophecy, and discerning of spirits. These may come as dreams including similitudes and dark speeches (Numbers 12:8), open vision, closed vision and intuition.

Dreams are highlighted in Job 33:15-16 as "visions of the night". That scripture says in a dream, in a vision of the night, when deep sleep falleth upon men, in slumberings upon the bed, then he openeth the ears if men and sealeth their instruction. However, dreams could be direct dreams in which case the dream happens just as it is seen in the dream, or it is symbolic (similitude), whereby a symbol is brought to you as an answer to your prayer. Praying for blessings may bring a fruitful tree in your dream, confirming you shall be like that tree based on Psalm 1:3.

The third type of dreams is the dark speech. This type of dream needs to be interpreted as is indicated in Job 33:23-24. Some of these "dark speech" dreams are reverse dreams. This means that when someone dreams of having a baby in the dream, or wedding in the dream, such people would find it difficult having a baby in real life, or wedding, as the case may be. Another example is when a child dreams about having a brilliant result in the dream about an exam, it usually means failure.

Colours too are relevant! A red ink on a result means failure, and a red uniform means affliction. Yellow colour means a bright glory, while purple means royalty or honour. A child could either be dreaming about red colour or could be dreaming about yellow. In this case, a child reaming about red colour needs extra attention, maybe in the area of health, or even academic performance.

Numbers that are written in the dream also bear significance, or the number of units of a particular object that you see. Sometimes, the name of a person you have known may help in interpreting a dream. If you pray about a particular situation overnight and in the dream, you have, you see an old friend called Joy, it means there would be Joy regarding the issue you are believing God for.

Furthermore, you might see a big tree with many fruits on it, in another dream. That is confirming in the spirit that the issue will be favourable.

Open and closed visions.

An open vision is the image or vision that you see when your eyes are wide open, and a closed vision is a vision that you see when your eyes are closed. Both visions may reveal direct information or come as dark speeches that still need interpretation. There are kids that have one of these, and are very accurate in context. However, it takes a good parent to discover these gifts and develop them through encouraging the child to share the visions whenever they see them. These gifts may be subdued if a child is not encouraged to use these gifts.

Intuition.

An intuition is an automatic understanding or knowledge of something, without the conscious use of reason, or analytical skills. One morning, I woke up at an unusually early time, around four in the morning, and the Holy Spirit told me to start preparing for work. I did and was off to work around 5.30 a.m. I later discovered that after I left for work, there was a dangerous fracas on my route in which there was a riot and many people were wounded.

In another example, I was passing in front of an electronic store and the spirit of God gave me a nudge to enter into that shop, which I did. As I went in, I decided to look around, until I saw a laptop that I had so desired for a long time, at a rock bottom price. I bought that computer and I have enjoyed it since then. Without explaining these phenomena to children, they won't know. The good thing however is that children are very inquisitive, and once you give them the know at a very early stage, they decide to learn how to use it.

In an intuition, you may have misplaced a thing, but without any analytical thinking or activation of memory, you head towards the chair by the garden, and you find it there! That is what an intuition does. Subconscious realisation of real truths or processes. There has been a hot debate over the phenomenon of intuition in psychology, but the Holy Spirit plays a prominent role in the development and manifestations of intuitions.

In another example, I boarded a luxury bus, from Mando, Kaduna, Nigeria, and was travelling to Lagos, Nigeria, during my youth service. I just felt uneasy and alighted from that bus without any clear reason. On the way to Lagos, I discovered that the initial bus that I alighted from had been involved in a ghastly accident. If you are calm enough and sensitive in the spirit, you feel an intuition deep in you a compulsion to act on something that defies explanation. I alighted from the bus without any logical reasoning or explanation, but just a nudge.

Discerning of spirits.

This is described in the bible as a spiritual gift. It helps to differentiate between Godly, human and demonic influences in spiritual matters. The main importance of the operation of this spirit is that it helps to truly know if a word, prophecy, vision or activity is Godly. With the gift of discerning of spirits, every evil work can be exposed. It is a gift that children can cultivate if they are taught.

The role of prayer in fulfilling the destiny of a child.

Prayer is communication with God. When we talk about communication, it is a two-way thing as God is interested in relating and speaking with us. Unfortunately, man likes to talk to God without expecting a word. However, the bible says in Psalm 19:2 that day unto day uttereth speech and night unto night sheweth knowledge. In Psalm 107:20, the bible also says, he sent his word, and headed them and delivered them from their destructions.

We need to receive God's instructions (2 Timothy 3:16) in order to make the best out of the destiny of a child. The only way by which we can do this is to communicate with God. There are however different kinds of prayers that we can pray to help a child. They are as follows;

Prayers of forgiveness and mercy.

Human beings are prone to commit sin, and the sins we commit is the power of the devil over mankind. In Luke 10:19, Jesus gives us authority over serpents and scorpions and every power of the enemy, confirming that nothing shall by any means hurt us.

We need to always pray for forgiveness of our sins, as we try not to commit sin. We need to pray for forgiveness of our sins as parents and as well teach our children to pray for forgiveness of their sins, making them to know why sin is dangerous and what unconfessed sin can cause in our lives.

Breaking of covenants.

There are different covenants operating against children that could affect their manifestations and greatness. This includes marine covenants, environmental covenants, inherited covenants, placental covenants, idol covenants, blood covenants, familiar spirit covenants, witchcraft covenants, birth covenants, and many others.

A covenant is a linkage between you and demonic spirits. In as much as covenants are in place, they wouldn't allow great things to show up in a life. Evil covenants are very powerful and pull back people from their manifestations.

Breaking of curses.

A curse is a consequence of sin and wrong doing in words, actions or deeds. A curse could be responsible for sickness, poor memory, family poverty, or the progress of the child in a mysterious manner. A curse could also affect the school, or teachers, thereby affecting the student's academic progress.

Breaking of evil dedication.

Children may have been dedicated to idols when they were born, or afterwards. Evil dedication yokes a child to an evil deity, surrounding the child by demons and increasing his vulnerability. Evil dedication means Evil powers are in control of the life of a child and could negatively control the child all his life if not dealt with. Strange behaviour is common in a child who has a yoke of evil dedication.

Pray for revelation.

In aspiring to be great in life, discovery through revelation is of utmost importance. The exact gifts of a child are known through revelation. The type of vocation a child should pursue, or the school where the child should pursue it is through revelation. It gives clarity as to why you were created, and the pursuits you need to align with in life. Revelation is key in every decision of a parent.

Pray for favour.

Favour is the approval, support, or liking for something or someone. A child who receives a scholarship is enjoying favour. My daughter received a straight scholarship to pursue her undergraduate program in a private university in Nigeria, was God's favour.

I received a postgraduate scholarship the following year to come to the United Kingdom, was favour too. When you receive favour, things that seemingly are difficult for others are easy for you. Exemption from one fee or the other that needs to be paid in school is favour. Anyone who prays for favour receives favour from men and angels.

Pray for wisdom.

An excellent application of knowledge is wisdom, and it brings good judgement and ability to be able to make good decisions. Wisdom is necessary if a child must make excellent choices, not just for the child, but the parents need to pray for wisdom as well. Wisdom is also necessary in passing exams.

Apart from praying, wisdom in children also could be developed through storytelling, discussions and reflection, mentorship and role modelling, as well as the introduction of real world and complex issues that require brainstorming and deep thinking.

Pray for a retentive memory.

A retentive memory is a valuable asset to any student. No matter how wise you may be, if your memory is not retentive, you tend to lose information too quickly. As the child prays, make sure they sleep well, are not stressed up, have a good nutrition, and exercise regularly. Regular physical activity promotes better blood flow to the brain and promotes cognitive function.

Pray for healing from underlying diseases.

Disease is an enemy of academic development or other types of achievement. It is good to pray against sicknesses and pray for healing and good health. Certain neurological disorders could affect memory, like Attention Deficit Hyperactivity Disorder (ADHD).

Pray for regional peace.

There can be no progress if there is no peace in the society. When there is unrest, the children cannot go to school. Even if they attend, the minds of everyone won't be at peace.

CHAPTER 11

PRAYERS TO DIG OUT HIDDEN POTENTIALS

Prayers for forgiveness and mercy.

O Lord, forgive me every sin in my thoughts in the name of Jesus Christ.

O Lord, forgive me every sin as a result of vain words that the enemy may likely use against me in the name of Jesus Christ.

I ask for forgiveness by the power in the blood of Jesus, concerning any sin in my activities that I have committed.

Foundational iniquity, be erased by the power in the blood of Jesus Christ.

Every evil spirit in my life, as a result of sin, loose me and let me go in the name of Jesus Christ.

I refuse to be partakers of the sin of my proprietors, and teachers in the name of Jesus Christ.

Inherited consequences of sin, be taken away by the power in the blood of Jesus Christ.

O Lord, in any way that I have refused to cooperate with teachers in class, forgive me in the name of Jesus Christ.

Prayers to break evil covenants.

I break every witchcraft covenant over my progress in life in the name of Jesus Christ.

Covenants and soul ties, stealing from me, break and release me now in the name of Jesus Christ.

Evil agreement with any idol power in my ancestral line, be cancelled by the power in the blood of Jesus Christ.

Witchcraft covenant hindering my destiny, release my destiny in the name of Jesus Christ.

Environmental covenant affecting my academic glory, be broken by the power in the blood of Jesus Christ.

I break and release myself from covenants with mind blinding spirits in the name of Jesus Christ.

Resurrection and the life, envelope my brain in the name of Jesus Christ.

Every unconscious agreement in my life entered in error, break and release me by the power in the blood of Jesus Christ.

Covenant of infirmity, break and release me in the name of Jesus Christ.

Covenant of failure at the edge of success, break and release me in the name of Jesus Christ.

Generational covenant of non-achievement in my family line, your time is up, break in the name of Jesus Christ.

Covenant with shame and reproach, break and release me in the name of Jesus Christ.

Covenant of stagnancy, break and release my life in the name of Jesus Christ.

Covenant of disaster that I entered into on the day of my birth, break and release me in the name of Jesus Christ.

Covenant assigned to cut short my glory, be broken in the name of Jesus Christ.

Every anti-success covenant, break and release me in the name of Jesus Christ.

Covenant of untimely and sudden death, break and release me in the name of Jesus Christ.

Evil power supervising any covenant in my life, I break your power, in the name of Jesus Christ.

Blood covenant in my foundation, break in the name of Jesus Christ.q

Prayers to break curses.

Every curse fashioned against my academic progress, break in the name of Jesus Christ.

Ancestral curse working against the greatness of glorious children in my family line, break in the name of Jesus Christ.

Environmental curse around my house, working against my glory, break in the name of Jesus Christ.

Environmental curse around my school, break in the name of Jesus Christ.

Curse of poverty assigned to stop my progress in life, break in the name of Jesus Christ.

Curse of generational infirmity affecting my family line, break in the name of Jesus Christ.

Pattern of the tail, operating in my family line, scatter in the name of Jesus Christ.

Every curse attacking the manifestation of God's talents and gifts in my life, break in the name of Jesus Christ.

Curse, chasing away helpers from me, break in the name of Jesus Christ.

Every curse working against my brain, break in the name of Jesus Christ.

Evert cursed equipment in my school, receive deliverance in the name of Jesus Christ.

Every curse working against my teacher's ability, break in the name of Jesus Christ.

Evil altars, cursing my life, receive destruction in the name of Jesus Christ.

Curse of limitation, fashioned against my potentials, break in the name of Jesus Christ.

Curse of debilitating illness, break and release me in the name of Jesus Christ.

I recover everything that I have lost as a result of curses in the name of Jesus Christ.

Curse of affliction targeted against my destiny, break in the name of Jesus Christ.

Every curse waiting to manifest on the day of my glory, break in the name of Jesus Christ.

Arresting curses working against my progress, break in the name of Jesus Christ.

Every curse programmed against my dwelling place, break and release me in the name of Jesus Christ.

Prayers to break evil dedication.

Evil linkage between me and any evil power in the forest, be broken in the name of Jesus Christ.

I redeem my life by the power in the blood of Jesus from every spiritual bondage in the name of Jesus Christ

Evil spiritual mark upon my life by virtue of any evil dedication, be wiped off by the power in the blood of Jesus Christ.

I release my glory, from the cage of evil dedication in the name of Jesus Christ.

Demonic spirits, supervising evil dedication in my life, be arrested in the name of Jesus Christ.

Wicked cord of evil dedication, joining me with any person, break and release me in the name of Jesus Christ.

Evil padlock of satanic dedication, affecting my thinking, break and release me in the name of Jesus Christ.

Anything that evil dedication has stolen away from my life, be restored in the name of Jesus Christ.

My dream life, refuse to cooperate with the power of evil dedication in the name of Jesus Christ.

I rise above every evil limitation by the power in the blood of Jesus Christ.

Evil garment put upon my life as a result of evil dedication, be removed in the name of Jesus Christ.

I reverse any evil impact upon my life by evil dedication in the name of Jesus Christ.

Evil hand of evil dedication upon my life, causing difficulty and hardship, wither in the name of Jesus Christ.

Evil dedication in my life, working with the cycle of the moon, break and release me in the name of Jesus Christ.

Every pet, dedicated to the devil in my surrounding, that is monitoring my destiny, be arrested by the Holy Ghost fire.

Any implied curse upon my life as a result of evil dedication, break and release me in the name of Jesus Christ.

Spirit responsible fur strange behaviour in my life, I break your power in the name of Jesus Christ.

Inherited evil dedication overshadowing my destiny, loose me and let me go in the name of Jesus Christ.

I block every evil pipe linking my life with evil altars, by the power in the name of Jesus Christ.

Every spirit of error, as a result of evil dedication, loose me and let me go in the name of Jesus Christ.

Altar of evil dedication assigned against my greatness, be broken and be destroyed by fire in the name of Jesus Christ.

Prayers for revelation and guidance.

O Lord, show me who I am in the name of Jesus Christ.

Father Lord, show me the gifts and talents that you have deposited in my life in the name of Jesus Christ.

Any decision or step that I have taken, that is not according to your will for my life, O Lord, expose it in the name of Jesus Christ.

My father and my God, show me the school that you have ordained to bring out the best in me in the name of Jesus Christ.

O Lord, show me the deep causes of my affliction in the name of Jesus Christ.

O Lord my father, show me the picture of the future that you have planted for me in the name of Jesus Christ.

Every dangerous enemy in the boat of my destiny, be exposed and be disgraced in the name of Jesus Christ.

O Lord, you changed the name of Jacob to Israel, show me my new name in the name of Jesus Christ.

Father, reveal to me the weakness of the enemy in the name of Jesus Christ.

My father, my father, establish your covenant of prosperity and good success in my life in the name of Jesus Christ.

O Lord my father, let your Holy spirit lead me and guide me all the days of my life in the name of Jesus Christ.

My father and my God, guide me to the place of huge success in my life in the name of Jesus Christ.

That mentor that will take me to my promised hand, O Lord, let me locate him, and let him locate me in the name of Jesus Christ.

O Lord my father, show me deep and secret things about my journey in life in the name of Jesus Christ.

O Lord, show me the secret of manifesting abundance in my life in the name of Jesus Christ.

I receive the revelation to receive excellent health all the days of my life in the name of Jesus Christ.

Every trap set for me by the enemy, be exposed and be disgraced in Jesus Christ name.

Any spirit in my life, disturbing the revelation of God, be disgraced by fire in the name of Jesus Christ.

Evil spirit, attacking my potentials, be exposed and be bound in the name of Jesus Christ.

Veil of darkness preventing me from knowing God's will for my life, be destroyed by the Holy Ghost fire in the name of Jesus Christ.

O Lord, reveal to me every mistake and weakness of my ancestors in the name of Jesus Christ.

Prayers for divine favour.

O God arise, and show me favour, in the journey of my destiny in the name of Jesus Christ.

Anti-favour covenant in my life, break by the power in the blood of Jesus Christ.

I break and release myself from the power of evil dedication that is saying no to God's favour in my life in the name of Jesus Christ.

Every curse that is assigned to cut me off from divine favour, break in the name of Jesus Christ.

Door of favour that's closed against my life, open by fire in the name of Jesus Christ.

Aroma of divine favour, be released upon my life in the name of Jesus Christ.

Powers destroying good things in my life, be arrested in the name of Jesus Christ.

O Lord, put upon my life, the garment of divine favour in the name of Jesus Christ.

I speak favour upon the life of my educational sponsors in the name of Jesus Christ.

Agenda of darkness to truncate God's favour in my life, be exposed and be disgraced in the name of Jesus Christ.

O Lord my father, relocate me if I need to be relocated to receive divine favour in the name of Jesus Christ.

I receive international favour in my educational pursuits in the name of Jesus Christ.

O Lord, open a new chapter of favour in my life in the name of Jesus Christ.

Aroma of God's favour, be released upon my life in the name of Jesus Christ.

I receive the mark of divine favour upon my life in the name of Jesus Christ.

Evil association robbing me of God's benefits for my life, scatter by fire in the name of Jesus Christ.

Anti-favour imagination and thoughts in my life, scatter by fire in the name of Jesus Christ

Voice of disfavour in my life, be silenced in the name of Jesus Christ.

Every enemy of God's favour in my life, be exposed and be disgraced in the name of Jesus Christ.

Witchcraft embargo working against my success in life, be lifted in the name of Jesus Christ.

Spirit of the living God, lead me to my place of divine favour in the name of Jesus Christ.

Every parental pronouncement working against my greatness, lose your power in the name of Jesus Christ.

I reject every spirit of error in the name of Jesus Christ.

Prayers for wisdom.

I receive the mantle of God's wisdom in the name of Jesus Christ.

Anointing of wisdom, fall upon my life in the name of Jesus Christ.

Negative thoughts, working against God's wisdom in my life, clear away by fire in the name of Jesus Christ.

I drink from the well of divine wisdom in the name of Jesus Christ.

Witchcraft arrow fired against my mind, come out by fire in the name of Jesus Christ.

Disorder of imagination in my life, be healed in the name of Jesus Christ.

Baptism of the Holy Ghost, fall upon my life in the name of Jesus Christ.

Any mental illness growing in my brain, be uprooted in the name of Jesus Christ.

I receive the gift of the word of wisdom in the name of Jesus Christ.

I receive the gift of interpretation of tongues in Jesus Christ name.

I receive the gift of discernment in the name of Jesus Christ.

Evil ancestral voice in my life, be silenced in the name of Jesus Christ

Evil influence in my life, assigned to mislead me, clear away in the name if Jesus Christ.

Spirit of wisdom, baptise my parents for excellent decisions in the name of Jesus Christ.

Counsellors that are ordained to support my life, locate my destiny in the name of Jesus Christ.

Every bewitchment of my brain, be reversed in the name of Jesus Christ

Angels of wisdom, intervene in every affair of my life in the name of Jesus Christ.

I receive a double portion of Solomon's wisdom for excellent in my journey of destiny in the name of Jesus Christ.

Every arrow of error, I command you to jump out of my life in the name of Jesus Christ.

Anointing to utter wise words, baptise my tongue in the name of Jesus Christ.

Prayers for a retentive memory.

Every spirit of forgetfulness, depart from me in the name of Jesus Christ.

Every cloud of confusion, over my brain, clear away by fire in the name of Jesus Christ.

Arrow of disaster and tragedy, assigned against my memory, come out by fire in the name of Jesus Christ.

I refuse to be a victim of stress in the name of Jesus Christ.

I receive healing from every illness affecting my memory in the name of Jesus Christ.

Every curse attacking my memory, break in the name of Jesus Christ.

Sacrifice on the road junction, against my memory, lose your power in the name of Jesus Christ.

Every evil word or declaration made against my memory, I break your power in the name of Jesus Christ.

I release my brain from the captivity of every evil altar in the name of Jesus Christ.

Every food that I need to stop eating that will help my retentive memory, be revealed to me in the name of Jesus Christ.

Every food and liquid that I need to start taking that will help my memory, be revealed unto me in the name of Jesus Christ.

Holy Spirit, incubate my brain for a retentive memory in the name of Jesus Christ.

Any environmental influence within or outside my school, that is affecting my retentive memory, be exposed and be disgraced in the name of Jesus Christ.

Padlock of witchcraft, fashioned against my brain, break, break, break in the name of Jesus Christ.

Rags of intellectual poverty, fashioned against my life, catch fire and burn to ashes in the name of Jesus Christ.

O Lord, lay your hands of deliverance upon my head, and let every yoke of memory loss be broken in the name of Jesus Christ.

Any embargo of witchcraft placed upon my retentive memory, be lifted in the name of Jesus Christ

I come out of every dark room of memory loss in the name of Jesus Christ.

Light of God, illuminate my mind in the name of Jesus Christ.

Every evil covenant in my life, affecting my memory, be broken by the power in the blood of Jesus Christ.

Inherited memory disaster in my family line, be exposed and be disgraced in the name of Jesus Christ.

Prayers for good health.

Seed of infirmity in my body, be destroyed by fire in the name of Jesus Christ.

O God, expose and disgrace every disease in my body, assigned to stop my academic success in the name of Jesus Christ.

Arrow of incurable disease, searching for my life, wither by fire in the name of Jesus Christ.

O Lord my father, reveal to me the solution to my stubborn health problems.

Every trap of infectious disease set for me, or my household, be destroyed by fire in the name of Jesus Christ.

Covenant of infirmity, fashioned against my life, break in the name of Jesus Christ.

Curse of infirmity, break and release me by the power in the blood of Jesus Christ.

Every dedication to any demon of sickness, break and release me in the name of Jesus Christ.

I receive deliverance from every embargo of sickness upon my life in the mighty name of Jesus Christ.

Garment of sickness upon my life, catch fire and burn to ashes in the name of Jesus Christ.

Chain of infirmity, break and release my life in the name of Jesus Christ.

Strongman of infirmity, lose me and let me go in the name of Jesus Christ.

Evil load of infirmity upon my life, I shake you off by fire in the name of Jesus Christ.

I break the yoke of any sickness that wants to stop me on my examination day in the name of Jesus Christ.

I decree that any disorder in my life that is stealing away my marks, be uprooted from my life in the name of Jesus Christ.

I cut myself off from the chain of infirmity, in my family line in the name of Jesus Christ.

Chain of sickness assigned to tie down my destiny, break in the name of Jesus Christ.

Environmental covenant of infirmity in my school, break in the name of Jesus Christ.

I walk out of the bondage of infirmity in the name of Jesus Christ.

Serpent of sickness, attacking me in the dream, catch fire and release me in the name of Jesus Christ.

I wash my destiny free from every yoke of infirmity in the name of Jesus Christ (Wash your head with the anointing oil)

Padlock of disability prepared for my life, by witchcraft, break and scatter in the name of Jesus Christ.

I receive healing from every disease of the eyes in the name of Jesus Christ.

I receive healing from every disorder of hearing in the name of Jesus Christ.

I command the demon of infirmity to jump out of my body in the name of Jesus Christ.

Prayers for regional peace.

Blood sucking and flesh-eating demons in charge of wars and unrest, working against our country, be silences in the name of Jesus Christ.

Every altar of violence in my region, I pull you down in the name of Jesus Christ.

Every rage of the wind of destruction fashioned against my school, be silenced in the name of Jesus Christ.

The sun shall not smite me by day nor the moon by night in the name of Jesus Christ.

Every curse, issued against my school, break in the name of Jesus Christ.

Environmental evil covenant fashioned against my environment, break in the name of Jesus Christ.

I arrest every fire disaster in my environment in the name of Jesus Christ.

I decree peace and tranquillity upon this environment in the name of Jesus Christ.

Let the altar of stubborn pandemic in my environment, be destroyed in the name of Jesus Christ.

Environment rage assigned against my society be dashed in the name of Jesus Christ.

Holy Spirit, intervene and stop every looming political instability in my environment in the name of Jesus Christ.

Demonic spirit, inspiring disaster and tragedy in my environment, be arrested in the name of Jesus Christ.

Every activity and plan of insurgents followed in my area, be foiled in the name of Jesus Christ.

Angels of the living God, guard and protect my environment in the name of Jesus Christ.

Power of evil dedication, working against my dwelling place, be destroyed in the name of Jesus Christ.

Power of rumours assigned to cause confusion in my school and environment, be disgraced in the name of Jesus Christ.

Shield of protection of the almighty fall upon me and my family in the name of Jesus Christ.

Spirit of the living God, let there be peace and let every communal conflict be settled in the name of Jesus Christ.

Every ritual sacrifice offered on any evil altar in my community assigned to caused unrest, break in the name of Jesus Christ.

Wicked altars in my country, promoting evil plans and intentions, be destroyed by fire in the name of Jesus Christ.

Satanic rage in the heavenlies against my destiny, be dashed in the mighty name of Jesus Christ

Covenant of infirmity unto death in my life, break by the power in the blood of Jesus Christ.

I reject sudden and untimely death in the mighty name of Jesus Christ.

Altar of witchcraft pandemic in my community, be destroyed by fire in the name of Jesus Christ.

Territorial armed robbers on assignment against our regional peace, be disgraced in the name of Jesus Christ.

Father I thank you, for there shall be peace in our nation.

Printed in Great Britain
by Amazon